Anniversaries and Afterimages

Anniversaries
and
Afterimages

Walter Gordon

WRITER'S PROOF

Published by Writer's Proof,
an imprint of Interview You, LLC
Athens, Georgia
www.interviewyou.net

The poems "*Chanson Innocente*" and "Wedding" have previously been published together as "*Chansons Innocentes*" in the *Anglican Theological Review*.

ISBN 978-0-9822726-1-9

Printed in the United States of America

For Julia

Order of Reading

Afterimages

The reality of love is mutilated when it is detached from all its unrealness.

—Gaston Bachelard

Introduction

My wife, Marjorie, died very suddenly of cardiac arrest at the age of sixty-six. At one moment on that late afternoon of June 11, 2002, we sat dozing at the living room table. Then, without warning, she began to writhe in those stark movements by which the body withstands the encroachment of death. I gave her what pitiful support I could to help her resist that awful grip. To no avail. Her teeth clenched, and my breath could no longer find a way of sustaining hers.

After she had gone, like so many who have suffered this worst of losses, I regretted not having told her what lay deepest in my heart about my feeling for her. As she grew older, I wanted to tell her that she had become more beautiful, but I could never find the words that would capture what I meant. Something that the younger woman only promised had reached fulfillment in her face, especially her eyes. The sign of her habitual way of giving had come to surface there. She looked outward, and gladly so, toward others, toward her child, toward her husband.

This regret over my silence about something she would have loved to have heard from me lingered in my mind late into the night following her demise. Then I remembered the poems I had written for her on the occasion of our wedding anniversaries. These were, if nothing else, attempts to express what I felt. I went looking and found them in the second drawer of her night stand. In reading through the verses, I began to feel grateful that I had tried to say something about the beauty of this woman.

Thoughts entered my mind about publishing the poems because I did not want her presence to pass unnoticed. To be sure, there have been others like her, but I did not know or love them intimately. Her I did, and my sense of that presence is set down in the words that follow. The writing consists of a mixture of the slight and the spacious, of the playful and the serious. I include all because our relationship is made of such things. The lines were meant for her. Now I submit them to the eyes of others after some revision. Whatever is good here derives from Marjorie's beauty.

WALTER GORDON

Dedication

What was it?
the thing I could not do
I did.

I wonder what to be's to do
now that to be is done.

You are my being-keep
you be me,
when I am not myself
you are.

I wrote this book
out of your being
what you do:

the complement
the nonesuch who
makes one
out of a disparate two.

Alone, the words
that follow
never would have come.

Anniversaries

Bouquet

Chrysanthemum, a budding flower,
for Marjorie
the girl

Chrysanthemum, a precious flower,
for Marjorie
the pearl

Chrysanthemum, a golden flower,
for Marjorie
the sun

Chrysanthemums, a bunch of flowers,
for Marjorie
the one.

Definition

Wedding:
a pledge
not unlike the warrior's promise
to follow out a long campaign
over razed fields into unknown lands;

a gage
that assures one's presence
at the trial by arms;

a wager
to wage
as men wage wars
to prove their innocence,

and yet
to stake no claim
to claim no booty
but bootless
to engage.

Firelight

There in the dark
I see where she waits
and her face lights
at the first of the evening's fireflies.

Woodland magic:
sparks without flint.
her eyes kindle
and, as with the tiny, winged creatures,
they rise slowly, silently
up the farther reaches of the pinewood
and the little rears of the flaming things
light a way to the star trails.

So from the conifers
her eyes move out again
up the galactic range
of the great flame carriers,
and like the old play's hero,
who rose to heaven on a beetle's back,
fly's fire catching in her eyes
mounts upward.

Sonus

Saying makes
say what you will
saying makes.

He spoke and all things
came to be.

There is a voice I know
it sings when she talks
it is a homing sound
that I home to
a joyful sound
that I rise to,
as she creates
when before there was nothing.

A Spire

You are the quick of my will
and quicker still.
You stretch for my want
and strain me,
fasten me
to my best desire.

In dark times
you light me,
daylike and daring
reaching out
to rouse the night.

What I had only dreamt of
there you leave it
waiting.

Salinas

When we reached Salinas
not far from Castroville,
the artichoke capital of the world,
we got a room with a queen-sized bed
and my partner grew sportive
and giggled her way through two gimlets.

I wondered if I needed
any drink at all
with her to spike the atmosphere
with her eyes
and tumble all grown-up thought down
to girl play.

Wedding

Eyes charged with light
she dressed in white
like a child on communion day;
and for communion
they do pray
of arms, thighs, hands,
of minds.

A common measure for a dance
a union in the leap and stance
a wedding on communion day
when they to one another say:
this is my body.

Legend

Can you believe
that into the wood
for a virgin lap
the unicorn fled
and raced and raced
for a virgin lap
on which he would
in the wild wood
rest his head?
Can you believe?

Yesterday and Tomorrow

Tomorrow is St. Valentine's
and at the turn of the tide
a plane is going to whisper in
my once and future bride.

I'll bring the ring she gave to me
and flowers and bows and then
we'll kiss and play another game
and ring around again.

Sonus II

Do hearts sound?
do they join with speech?
do they transform words beyond meaning?

A voice is heard
that fills the air
and finds its way
through words
past sense and the visible.

Her voice
transforms sound
into spirit
as if words
were made
to turn themselves
into silence.

Hurricane

Billow down, belly up
the fifty-foot swell
in from the wind lash
in from the rain swirl
eye.

Fixture of heart floods
absence of rage
free from the roundabout
stillpoint of all without
you.

Keepsake

I will not keep you
women don't keep well
and yet I do.

I keep you
as children do their holidays
as hurdy-gurdies playing
as ballerinas time.

I keep you,
of thoughts I cannot keep the count,
in mind,

And in my weakness,
I would keep the whole of you
forever in my reach,

But you escape
leading a reckless chase
past sorrow, death, and doom
and all of me.

High and Low

Let her go
untouched
into the vastness
of space
beyond the breath
of moon desire.

My sunscraper
my star finder,
falcon,
flushing a new hunt

For the light
in the thicket
under the bush
under the bushel.

Astrologue

The gravity of things
the weight of wonder moons
under the hold of Jupiter.

The star-leader
of this high dance
in the age of alchemy
was thought to have been
love-driven.

We know better now
now we call it mass,
volume, weight, pull, thrust.

But the ancient doctor saw no difference
and joined the world of Jesus with our own:
pondus meum amor meus.

Comet fall and star rise

I have seen eyes
drawing mine into their sphere
and away she went
sky-searching:

I followed.

Chanson Innocente

Why do the little stars burn
Burn in the evening sky,
Race through the heavens and turn
In a galaxy dance way high?

Go follow the gist of this rune,
And the drift of the fires above
And bring me by sun or by moon
The Star whom the little stars love.

A Breath Away

Air breathed
becomes part of me
by some trick of the blood:

hot air paling me
cold air redd'ning me
the master element
the life of me
within me;

and yours too
an air
that wraps you
like breezes wrap planets
and wave palms.

The air of you, distilled
moves like music on waters.

My heart breathes you
without knowing
without seeing
inhaling life
by some trick of the blood.

Sonus III

Sounds, voices
audial reveries,
the spirit informs the voice
her speech is all soul
and her soul
mingles with mine.

One small voice
can fill my space
her word
echoes within.

The word that sounds me,
to the bone, to the quick,
to the inner room
the secret place
she fills.

Soundings

Wife,
when you speak, come to me,
do not vociferate from distant rooms
imagining you can toss
your voice through the house
like a football.

Still,
when you speak not
I listen
and wait upon the silences
when words turn to bodily movement
for the slow of hearing
and I watch out of fear
lest something you say will be lost
in the language you speak best:

Not the word vibrating
through the hall
but the sound become flesh
become sore
become love.

Revolution

The white breakers I hear
sounding in the distance,
night shore
day shore
they come again and again.
winds follow
up the sand,
drift and settle.

Nature leans
down its own way,
windward the palm trees
roundly the stones.

Your love mocks
this legal rate,
pitching its tent
in a campground
littered with unpredictables
neither you nor I
can sweep away.

So let us not straighten the mess
for callers,
but sit and play house
under a programmed moon
and stars that stand in queue.

Mysterium Lucis

Light
I was told
never rests
but moves,
unflaggingly,
chasing the darkness
to infinitude.

No plutonium here
nor gold,
that heavy element,
sluggish, retrievable,
fit for minting
and for wasting;

but light issues gently
out of unfathomable ions and atoms
to stir not a leaf
not a needle
not a web
mingling
with that other mystery
of light
rising out of your soul
into your eyes.

Sonus IV

Down in the garden
the rain falls
ever so gently
like the fall of her voice...
And a bird flies off
leaving silence and emptiness.

Words flutter
and flee upwind
for a long journey;

Words make soundings
down
into deep waters.

What sounds
beyond us
does love listen to?

Predestination

When you rose
out of nothingness
that destined
the whole of me.

Play

Playfellow
looking for seashells
to no purpose
wondering at the cat
mother-wise
cajoling him
to no end.

Children
when playing at grown-ups
tear down their house
and make it anew
to their size
and confuse the worrisome world
into a toy.

Three Words

I

think, for reasons known and unknown,
my body aches,
and my mind gropes
towards images
that flee from me.
I want to dream waking
a dream I will remember.

Love

grows out of fancy.
dreams mean more than
schedules, summonses, and
social calls,
more like children's tales
rendezvous and rituals.
They reach into the dark—
darkness undoes me,
disturbs my balance—
and dreams thrive in the night,
and even the daylight, waking ones
blind us, unmind us
for no one sees love's origin.

You

waken the dream
in ways foreign to me
and, lo, again the dark.
you are the mystery
so I must needs pray
the Silent One
calling me to say
something far more blessed
than this cross tongue can speak.

Repose

We sense it in the light
that bathes the solitary girl
in Vermeer;

We feel it at that point
when the music
stays its movement.

You might call it nothing
the mind's nada
the space
where all souls flee
as to deliverance
from judgment.

I speak of silences
holy men say with;
I speak of yours
a silence, a stay-with.

I speak of you,
the best of you,
the quintessential
rest of you.

Summer Winds

The summer winds had not yet reached us
they were still at sea
leaving us time to build sand castles;

and there the water lay
like some untold future
stretching out to a settlement
with the far heaven at the horizon.

The trees now grow
weary of the skies
and with the redd'ning color comes
the dimming of the eyes.

And do I know now
what I saw then?
(or do we ever see?)
the journey-woman, first and last,
and my best company.

Communion

The philosopher tells us
That the fullness of marriage
is had
in a union of souls
so that after our two bodies
couple
we just might turn out
to be friends.

There's graciousness in that:
settling on the down
to become bedfellows
who share each other's
rest:

Breathing together
as one,
inspiring
One Spirit,
The aspiration
of all flesh.

Afterimages

Manners

I did not know
that you would soon be leaving
and that this would be
the last day
that we would share together.

I had no inkling
that you would go
without so much
as one embrace
like one who'd not been taught
her manners
nor how to say good-bye.

But on the day you left
the silence of the clock
in just that instant
became a measure
of all the days of servitude
I wasted on myself
the unresponsive lover
more mannerless than you.

Presence

And were she there
in the very next room
I might turn to go
where she stood still

or, silent, I might listen to
her presence
through the walls,
hers now a spirit
made known
only through senses
that have been touched
by some higher frequency

But no. If I did think her here
I would not wonder where.
She walks not through these halls
she haunts not any room
the place co-heres in her.

In Aeternum

I had watched her fall asleep
I know not how many times.
It all came so naturally
That I took little notice
Of her eyes when they shut.
It was her way of tokening
A loss of interest.
Suddenly the world around her
Had simply gone away.

Where had she set her eyes?
What darling drew her heart?

She told me once
A cold, recurring dream
Of driving the freeway into the coming lane
I reached as if to save her
But such was not my role—
A turn perhaps, toward life,
And that once made
She finds my eyes
The image of her own:
The dark that hides in every dimming light,
Face to face with her own disappointment.

Is it not strange
That in such gloom
The breath of love
Hides within our weakness:
The never-chill,
The never-cease,
What we want most
To never waste?

Vision

I saw her today
out of the corner of my eye
as if, like the furniture,
she would always be here.

I saw her today
like the afterimage
we see
with eyes shut,
but today mine were open
and the pressure of a light
still rubbed against
my weakened retina.

I saw her today
and then she was gone
all in a second
and her going made me wonder
if what I'd seen
had stolen from my mind,
a counterfeit of what I still
do search for;
or was it light
sheer light
to tell me I am blind?

Exit

What was it that left
when her light went out?

She had a way of walking
that seemed to mock
her own depths.

At home she would amble
in her loose-fitting clothes
careless and indecorous
the antithesis of fashion;
and thus attired
she'd pass you by
and you would never guess
the fullness of her presence.

Why she could walk straight
into a heart
and without flinching,
close the door
and settle there.

About the Author

Walter Gordon taught English literature for five years at Loyola-Marymount University and for twenty-eight years at the University of Georgia, where he retired as professor emeritus. He has one daughter, Julia.

In addition to published articles and poems, Gordon is the author of the book *Humanist Play and Belief: The Seriocomic Art of Desiderius Erasmus*. He currently is completing a book about violence in the works of Thomas More.